THE ULTIMATE
1099 GUIDE

For Entrepreneurs Who
Give and Receive 1099's

STEPH WYNNE

Cover design by: Steph Wynne

Skinny Books Publishing

THE IRS DELAYS FORM 1099-K Again!!

NEWS ALERT!
12-10-23

Yep, the IRS has decided to pause the implementation of Form 1099-K for 2023.

What this means is that, for 2023, the IRS is reverting to the previous threshold. Anyone earning $20,000 or more and conducting 200 or more transactions will receive a 1099-K in January 2024.

This older requirement is now back in effect for 2023.

If the IRS had implemented the new law, starting in January 2024, most businesses and individuals would likely have received a 1099-K.

A similar delay occurred last year, but it was on December 22, 2022, just before Christmas, when the IRS quietly announced the delay of the 1099-K for 2022.

Now, beginning in 2024, the threshold will be set at $5,000. This means that in 2024 if you were paid through a third party like Venmo, Paypal, Square, Cash App, or numerous others, you will receive one or more 1099-K forms in 2025.

I have a strong feeling that the $5,000 threshold will remain in place for 2024 and beyond, rather than the $600 threshold that the IRS had originally intended to implement.

So, let's rejoice and be happy!

For more information directly from the IRS on Form 1099-K, visit their website.

- Steph

CONTENTS

Please note that the information provided in this guide is intended for general informational purposes only and should not be considered as tax advice.

1099-K INDIVIDUAL SUMMARY

Individuals may receive a 1099-K in four different situations:

1. When they receive a payment through a third-party platform (such as PayPal, Square, Cash App, etc.), and the money is deposited into their bank account. If the payment received is over $600, they will receive a 1099-K.

2. When they receive a payment through platforms like eBay, Amazon, Etsy, Shopify, SoundCloud, etc., and the money is deposited into their bank account. If the payment received is over $600, they will receive a 1099-K.

3. When they receive a payment for their services through platforms like Uber, Lyft, DoorDash, etc., and the money is deposited into their bank account. If the payment received is over $600, they will receive a 1099-K. However, they may also receive a 1099-K for any amount earned.

4. When they receive a payment through Zelle (which has no fees), and the money is deposited into their bank account. In this case, they will not receive a 1099-K from Zelle. However, it's important to note that Zelle is owned by a group of banks who may disclose deposit information to the IRS in the future.

An individual is someone who doesn't have a company. If you have gigs or side hustles you are an individual.

1099-K SELF-EMPLOYED SUMMARY

Self-employed may receive a 1099-K in four different situations:

1. If you sell products or services and receive payments through a merchant account, such as through your bank, and the total payments received are over $600, you will receive a 1099-K.

2. If you sell products or services and receive payments through a third-party processor like Paypal, Square, Venmo, Cash App etc. and the total payments received are over $600, you will receive a 1099-K.

3. If you sell products or services through online platforms like eBay, Amazon, Etsy, Shopify, SoundCloud, and the platform takes a fee and you receive over $600, you will receive a 1099-K.

4. If you sell products or services and receive payments through a third-party processor like Zelle, which does not charge a fee, you will not receive a 1099-K. However, it's worth noting that Zelle is owned by a group of banks who may have access to your deposit information in the future.

If doesn't matter if you are a sole proprietor, LLC, LLP, S. Corporation or Corporation.

Most Entrepreneurs Are Sole Proprietors

A sole proprietorship refers to an individual who owns and operates an unincorporated business on their own. This includes a range of businesses, such as mom-and-pop stores, local clothing boutiques, artists, writers, IT consultants, web designers, tattoo artists, book-keepers, photographers, plumbers, graphic designers, doctors, hair-stylists, makeup artists, online sellers, dentists, veterinarians, lawyers, accountants, electricians, contractors, subcontractors, and others.

Throughout this guide, we will use the terms business owner, entre-preneur, contractor, and self-employed interchangeably to refer to individuals who operate their own businesses.

What's It All About?

"Taxes are what we pay for a civilized society." U.S. Supreme Court Justice Oliver Wendell Holmes, Jr.

The above quote is engraved on the front of the IRS building in Washington, DC and sums up the purpose of taxes and why you need to pay your share.

Congress says, *"In order for our society to thrive, governments on all levels need funds for defense, security (police and fire), social services, education, infrastructure (roads, utilities and sewage), the court system, and more. In order for government services to be provided, different types of taxes are collected."*

An IRS analysis of 2014-2016 estimated that unreported individual and small business activities cost $144 billion in taxes a year, and found that Americans report less than half of the income that is not automatically reported for them, according to Bloomberg.

"I think the level of non-compliance from small businesses is staggering," says Steven Rosenthal, a senior fellow at the Urban-Brookings Tax Policy Center, told Bloomberg.

This is where you come in. You need to pay your share of taxes. The IRS and Congress are concerned that taxpayers are not reporting their full income and

What is a 1099?

therefore not paying their share of "worldwide" income taxes. To track income and ensure tax compliance, they rely on 1099 forms.

As a business owner, or third party processor you must file a 1099 form with the IRS to report payments made to the self-employed or individuals during the tax year that total over $600.

Three 1099s You Should Know About

Similar to how an employee receives a W-2 form, which their employer reports to the IRS, the 1099 form is used to report income to the IRS.

There are various types of 1099 forms, but you only need to be aware of three that report income:

The three main types of 1099 forms used to report income to the IRS are: the 1099-MISC, 1099-NEC, and the 1099-K, which is known to be problematic.

The 1099-MISC, short for "Miscellaneous", is used to report direct payments of $600 and was originally associated with payments made to self-employed individuals for products or services over $600.

However, it is now primarily used to report other income, such as rents, legal fees, royalties, prizes, or awards paid to individuals.

The 1099-NEC is used to report non-employee compensation, such as payments made to bookkeepers, accountants, freelancers, contract workers, consultants, and other business-to-business services, typically via physical check or wire transfer for payments over $600. This form has replaced the 1099-MISC for reporting non-employee compensation.

The 1099-K is the most problematic form, and many people complain about receiving it. It is usually received by individuals who are paid by a third-party processor like Square, Paypal, Stripe, Cashapp, Venmo, Etsy, eBay, Shopify, Amazon, and others.

It is worth noting that Zelle does not give out 1099-Ks, but it may not be entirely safe as it is owned by a group of banks who may eventually report your deposits to the IRS.

"The 1099 Forms are About Tracking Your Income"

Why is form 1099-K a problem?

With the new law of 2021 you don't have to be self-employed to get a 1099-K. It's important to know that both the buyer and the seller of services can get a 1099-K if they receive payments.

There are two scenarios that involve the use of 1099-Ks:

1. If you are paid for your services by a third party and the payment is over $600, you will receive a 1099-K.

2. If you pay someone for their services and the payment is over $600, the third party will give a 1099-K on your behalf.

Typically, the individual or business owner would not file a 1099-K themselves, as it is the responsibility of the third party payment platform or cash app to file it for them if they accept debit cards or use a third party payment platform to sell goods or services to customers.

CPA Practice Advisor contributor Mary Girsch-Bock wrote in June 2022 that the new 1099-K reporting requirements were snuck inside the American Rescue Plan Act that was passed in 2021.

If you're a small business owner and receive the majority of customer payments from cash, or checks, you'll likely be unaffected.

But if you use third party settlement organizations to get paid, the rules have changed. Beginning in 2024 (previously

"The Form 1099-K Will be the Most Hated Form on Earth!

What's all the fuss?

reported as 2023), companies such as PayPal, Square, Stripe, Venmo, and others will send a 1099-K form to individuals who receive over $600 in payments during the year.

Additionally, third-party settlement organizations like Airbnb, Uber, and Lyft will also issue 1099-Ks to individuals who have had multiple gigs with them.

The IRS and Congress are concerned about the amount of unpaid taxes and are taking steps to address the issue by tracking income worldwide.

To ensure tax compliance, they are requiring third-party payment processors to issue 1099-K forms for payments over $600 for goods and services via their apps, which are then filed directly with the IRS.

Before 2022, online companies that processed payments already issued 1099-Ks to sellers who exceeded 200 transactions or sales and $20,000 in income annually.

However, beginning in 2024, the income threshold will decrease from $20,000 to $600, with no minimum number of transactions required.

This means that if you received $600 or more for the sale of goods or services through third-party processors like eBay, Etsy, Amazon, Cash App, or payment services like Shopify, Stripe, Square, PayPal, and Venmo, you may receive a 1099-K in early 2024.

Even if you are just an occasional online seller of used household items or clothing. This threshold captures sellers running businesses and includes most people who were cleaning out their garages and closets.

"The 1099-K tax form will be more

"The Number One Tax Problem in 2023 Will be the 1099-K"

of a challenge for consumers who use online marketplaces to unload old goods or collectibles.

The new 1099-K reporting is going to cause questions and confusion for taxpayers who haven't received them before," said Kathy Pickering, chief tax officer at the Tax Institute at H&R Block.

"As a result, the sales of goods and services on personal accounts that shouldn't be taxable will be reported as taxable income by some 3rd party processors."

For example, in 2022 you held a garage sale and made an impressive $1,500 in sales. It was a relief to finally get rid of all that old stuff, and you probably didn't think about or know about reporting the income on your tax return, since you already paid sales tax on the items.

However, if you used a payment service like Cash App and sold an item for $900 to your neigh-bor George, you can expect to receive a 1099-K form in 2024. This form informs the IRS about the $900 payment, and they will expect you to report it on your tax return.

Even if you originally bought the item for more than you sold it for, such as a couch that you bought for $1,400 and sold for $900, which technically represents a loss, the payment service provider and the IRS will only see the payment of $900.

Therefore, you will need to prove to the IRS that the couch was sold at a loss to avoid paying taxes on the entire amount. The problem with 1099-Ks is that they indicate your revenue rather than your profit, which is the only taxable amount.

For example, if you sold used furniture for $900, the 1099-K would show $900 even if you spent much more to acquire the furniture.

"If You Receive a Payment for Your Products or Services You Will Receive a 1099"

t may be hard to believe, but this is just the beginning. If, in 2023, you pay your 17-year-old babysitter or the 16-year-old who mows your lawn a total of over $600 via a third-party payment processor, they will receive a 1099-K in 2024, despite their innocence in the matter.

What if the same scenario happened and you paid your babysitter or lawn guy with Zelle? "*Zelle, the payment app is owned by a group of big banks, and does not issue 1099-Ks,*" said spokeswoman, Meghan Fintland.

"*The law requiring some payment services to report transactions doesn't apply to Zelle, she said, because it is a bank-to-bank network and doesn't handle "settlement" of funds.*

But that doesn't mean that payments received via Zelle may not be taxable. "*It's up to the individual to handle their tax implica-*

tions. People will think there's a safe haven with Zelle," Ms. Fintland said.

Income is considered income, regardless of who receives it, and it is necessary to report it either by the minor or their parents. It has always been mandatory to declare and report any income, be it personal or business, when filing taxes, regardless of whether a tax form is generated or the method of payment used.

Therefore, even if your babysitter did not receive a 1099-K in prior years, any taxable income they earned through third-party payment platforms still had to be reported on their tax return or on their parents' income tax return.

However, Steven Rosenthal, a senior fellow at the Urban-Brookings Tax Policy Center, told Bloomberg. com he sees two likely outcomes if people continue to send and receive payments thinking they will evade taxes by using Zelle.

13

CONTINUED ON NEXT PAGE

"Crowd Funding is Income and is Taxable"

"Congress could extend the law to include Zelle, or the IRS could investigate customer names from Zelle for heightened auditing scrutiny. It's a dangerous game for tax cheats to migrate to Zelle," he said.

"It wouldn't be hard for the IRS to unravel that."

Self-Employed vs Employee

Business owners are advised by the IRS to accurately classify their workers as either employees or self-employed individuals.

Self-employed individuals typically operate in an independent trade, business, or profession and provide their services to the public. They often receive a 1099 form for their income received or for payments made for products or services.

On the other hand, an employee is anyone who provides services to a business owner and receives a W-2 form, regardless of the individual's degree of autonomy in performing their job.

The main distinction between self-employed individuals and employees is that the employer is responsible for submitting taxes directly to the IRS in the case of employees. Self-employed individuals, on the other hand, are expected to make quarterly estimated tax payments to the IRS, though many opt to pay annually.

Who are the Third Party Processors?

The American Rescue Plan Act that was signed into law in 2021. This new tax law requires *"third-party settlement organizations"* (TPSOs), such as PayPal, Stripe, Square, Venmo, Cash App and others to report the payments to the IRS of $600

"Nothing is Certain, Except Death and Taxes." Benjamin Franklin

or more in annual gross sales, regardless of the total number of transactions, on 1099-K forms.

Previously, this form was only given to users who received more than $20,000 and 200 transactions from selling goods and services in one year.

So who are the 3rd party processors? There are over 1,000, however below are the main ones:

Paypal (owns Venmo), Square, Stripe, Amazon, Etsy, eBay, Cash app, Uber, Lift, Coinbase, AirBnb, DoorDash, Shopify, Soundcloud, and many other 3rd party processors who paid you.

Zelle is a bank to bank processor and does not give 1099's. Don't be naive to think the IRS is gonna roller over and forget about the money you received through Zelle.

For sales over $600, TPSOs have to send out Form 1099-K. It's usually not clear whether casual sellers owe taxes on their sales. The change will be confusing, causing some people to pay taxes they don't owe. *"Millions of people could receive the 1099-K forms early next year,"* said Christopher Walters, chief executive of Blucora, the parent company of TaxAct do-it-yourself tax software. *"A lot of people are likely to be surprised,"* he said.

"The change is not meant to apply to people who are receiving payments as gifts or as reimbursements from friends after splitting the cost of a restaurant meal," said Erin Collins, the national taxpayer advocate, who heads an agency within the IRS that assists taxpayers.

"But some people could mistakenly receive 1099-K forms anyway if they get payments mislabeled as business transactions rather than friends and family payments," she said.

"Your Hobby Will be Taxed if You are Paid $600 or More.

"The IRS will not likely not know if a transaction is a reimbursement, gift or donation," said Brandenburg.

"The recipient should know this and can report any required items on their tax returns but should keep track of any items that do not need to be reported on their return in case they are ever asked about this."

How does the IRS know you even collected the money? Well if you use a 3rd party receive payments they will send the 1099-K to the IRS!

The IRS Hates Gigs and Side Hustlers

Many people are hustlin' and doing gig work on a part-time or full-time basis. Gig work can be driving a car, selling products or services online, even renting out your couch.

As the gig economy continues to grow, more people are turning to side hustles and gig work to supplement their income.

However, this trend has caused some tension with the IRS who are struggling to keep up with the changing nature of work in the modern economy.

The IRS hates gig workers and side hustlers for a number of reasons. For one, these individuals often work for multiple employers and receive income from a variety of sources, which can make it difficult for the IRS to track their earnings and ensure they are paying their fair share of taxes.

This has led to concerns that gig workers and side hustlers are not paying enough in taxes and could be contributing to a growing tax gap in the United States.

Another issue is that many gig workers and side hustlers are

"3rd Party Processors are the Gatekeepers For the IRS"

classified as independent contractors rather than employees.

This means that they are responsible for paying their own taxes and do not receive benefits such as health insurance, retirement plans, and paid time off.

While this arrangement can be beneficial for workers in some respects, it can also make it harder for the IRS to ensure that these individuals are paying the right amount in taxes and are not engaging in tax evasion or other illegal activities.

The IRS has also expressed concerns about the rise of cash-based transactions in the gig economy. Many gig workers and side hustlers are paid in cash, which can make it easier for them to under report their income and avoid paying taxes on their earnings.

This has led to increased scruti-

ny of cash transactions and more rigorous enforcement of tax laws in the gig economy.

Overall, the IRS's concerns about gig workers and side hustlers are not unfounded. As more people turn to gig work and side hustles to make ends meet, it is important for the government to ensure that everyone is paying their fair share of taxes.

While this may require some adjustments to the tax code and greater enforcement efforts on the part of the IRS, it is a necessary step to ensure the long-term stability of the U.S. economy and tax system.

1099-NEC Case Study:

"Are Business Owners Required to Give Contractors a W-9?"

MAX WILL SIGN A W9 BEFORE HE WORKS

For example Joe hires Max to design his website. Max will not get a form 1099-K. Max is a sole proprietor so Joe will give Max a W-9 before he starts work.

Even if Max is a gig worker Joe should give Max a W-9.

When Max fills out the W-9 he gives Joe his name, business name (if any), address and SS#. The W-9 is not sent to the IRS but stays in Max's file.

Of course some contractors feel like they don't need to fill out a W-9 but they do. You could get fined if they don't. Be firm about the W-9.

Max works from home and Joe

MAX WORKS HARD AS A INDY CONTRACTOR

...AND MAKES A LOT OF MONEY!

pays Max $12,300 with **business checks** for the year.

At the end of the year Joe will give Max a **1099-NEC** and a copy to the IRS.

This is how the IRS will know that Max received the $12,300. **So how does Joe report the 1099-NEC to the IRS?**

Joe could buy a 1099-NEC package from an office supply store such as Staples and have his bookkeeper process the 1099-NEC in-house with her printer.

But Joe shouldn't bother doing that when he can pay $5 for a company to process the 1099-NEC for him.

Since Joe has Max's info via the

"The IRS is Coming for the Gig Workers and Side Hustlers"

W-9 form, he has his bookkeeper process the 1099-NEC form.

The bookkeeper inputs Max's name (or business name) address, Social security number, EIN (employer identification number) or TIN (tax identification number) directly into the online form.

Pay $5 to process the 1099-NEC for Max and wala done! The online company will mail Max a 1099-NEC and will file the busi-

Why it's a
Headache

ness form 1096 for Joe. Max will receive the 1099-NEC in the mail no later than January 31, 2024.

Joe's bookkeeper will save a copy of the 1099-NEC for her files and send Max a PDF copy via email.

In this case study Joe is the **GIVER** of the 1099-NEC and Max

is the **RECEIVER** of the 1099-NEC. Joe would do this for every contractor or self-employed person he pays with a **check or cash** in 2023 paid at least $600.

What if Max wants to be paid using his Paypal account and Joe agrees?

Max will receive a 1099-K from Paypal.

Will Max still have to fill out a W-9?

Technically no, but Joe should ask for it to be kept on file.

Will Max get a 1099-NEC?
No.

What tax form will Max get?

That's right Max will get a 1099-K from Paypal showing all the payments from Joe to Max.

What if Max is also a driver for Uber or Lyft?

"Almost Everybody Will Get Some Sort of 1099"

Frequently Asked Questions

Q. Can I get more than one 1099?
Yes.

Q. Whose responsibility is it to make sure I get all my 1099's?
It's your responsibility.

Q. If I only get paid by checks will I get a 1099-K?
No. 1099-K 's are from 3rd party like Paypal, Venmo, Square etc.

Q. As a contractor am I required to fill out a W-9 if requested?
Yes.

Q. What are 3rd party processors?
A third-party processor allows businesses and individuals to accept card payments usually at flat-rate fees.

Q. How much money do you need to earn to receive a 1099?
$600

Q. Will the IRS know if I don't file a 1099?
If you received a 1099, the IRS knows so make sure you include it with your taxes.

Q. What is the 1099 Form Used for?
To report money you earned to the IRS.

Q. When will I receive my 1099 tax form?
By January 31st of every year

Q. How much can you pay someone without a 1099 in 2022?
Less than $400.

Q. What does it mean if I get a 1099?
The IRS knows about the money you got.

Q. Is a 1099 the same as W-2?
No. Employees get W-2s.

Q. Can I be a 1099 Employee?
Technically no such term exists from a legal standpoint. Since a person who received a 1099 can not be an employee some companies don't know and use the term to distinguish an employee from an independent contractor.

Who Gets a 1099?

Entity Type	Get a 1099?	Notes
Sole Proprietors	Yes	
LLC	Yes	No if the LLC files taxes as a corp
LLP	Yes/No	
S. Corporation	No	Yes, if an attorney 1099-MISC
Corporation	No	Yes, if an attorney 1099-MISC

Small Business	Entity Type	Amount Paid	Type of Possible 1099
Byron's Web Design	Sole Proprietor	$1,500	1099-NEC, 1099-K
Lock and Roll Movers, Inc.	Corporation	$3,312	1099-K if 3rd party processor is used
Bob and Larry's Repair Service	Partnership	$950	1099-K if 3rd party processor is used
Randy' Electrician Service	Sole Proprietor	$2,650	1099-NEC, 1099-K
Boston Bookkeeping Service, Inc.	S. Corporation	$12,060	1099-K if 3rd party processor is used
Kevin Clark Attorney At Law, Inc.	S. Corporation	$5,000	1099-NEC, 1099-K if 3rd party processor is used
Boston Legal Services, Inc.	Corporation	$1,200	1099-NEC, 1099-K if 3rd party processor is used
AT&T, Inc.	Corporation	$8,020	They could get a 1099-K but you will never know
Stuart A. Lindsey, CPA	Sole Proprietor	$2,500	1099-NEC, 1099-K
Arco Parking, LLP	Partnership	$7,500	1099-K if 3rd party processor is used
Barry's Computer Repair Service	Sole Proprietor	$795	1099-NEC, 1099-K
Andersen and Rogers, Law Firm	Partnership	280,000	1099-K if 3rd party processor is used
Angie's Catering Service, LLC	S. Corporation	$850	1099-K if 3rd party processor is used

Corporations and LLPs normally don't not get 1099's, however lawyers are the exception if paid legal fees and will get a 1099-NEC. A corporation or LLP can get a 1099-K if they use a 3rd party processor.

"Make Sure You Track Who Pays You and How"

He'll get a 1099-K from them as well!

If Joe were to give Max a 1099-NEC Max will be taxed twice and really mad! This is a real situation that can and probably will happen.

It's up to Max to stay on top of his gigs. Max could have ten 1099's if he has a lot of gigs and side hustles going on.

Max must make sure he gets all his 1099-K's. Some of Max's clients pay him by check so he will

This is way too confusing!

get the 1099-NEC. Max could even get a W-2 if he works as an employee.

It's important that Max checks each of his 3rd party accounts for

a 1099-K as they might not tell him.

This will be the number one problem in 2024 that contractors will deal with. Don't get confused. The IRS just wants to make sure Max's income is reported.

If Max does not report all his income he will get an AUDIT BILL from the IRS!

Examples: Find a Situation Similar to Yours

*Everybody will get a 1099-K for payments over $600
if a 3rd Party Processor was used

Products or Service on-line or off-line	Entity Type	3-Party payments	Cash or check	1099 type likely to be received. You can get more than one 1099
Web designer	Sole Proprietor	Yes	Yes	1099-NEC/1099-K
Etsy, eBay seller	Sole Proprietor	Yes	No	1099-K
Shopify seller	Sole Proprietor	Yes	No	1099-K
Bookkeeper	Sole Proprietor	Yes	Yes	1099-NEC/1099-K
Attorney	Sole Proprietor	Yes	Yes	1099-NEC/1099-K
Writer	Sole Proprietor	Yes	No	1099-K
Graphic Designer	Sole Proprietor	Yes	No	1099-NEC/1099-K
IT Tech Guy	Sole Proprietor	Yes	Yes	1099-NEC/1099-K
Plumber	Sole Proprietor	Yes	Yes	1099-NEC/1099-K
Instagram Influencer	Sole Proprietor	Yes	No	1099-K
Shopify	Sole Proprietor	Yes	No	1099-K
B&L Repair Service	LLP	Yes	Yes	1099-K
Randy' Electric	Sole Proprietor	Yes	Yes	1099-NEC/1099-K
Mario's Cabinets	Sole Proprietor	Yes	Yes	1099-NEC/1099-K
Mechanic Service	Sole Proprietor	Yes	No	1099-K
Hustler	Sole Proprietor	Yes	No	1099-K
Babysitter	Sole Proprietor	Yes	No	1099-K
Driver	Sole Proprietor	Yes	No	1099-K
Handyman	Sole Proprietor	Yes	Yes	1099-NEC/1099-K
Podcaster	Sole Proprietor	Yes	No	1099-K
Hair Stylist	Sole Proprietor	Yes	No	1099-K
Fitness trainer	Sole Proprietor	Yes	No	1099-K
Accountant	Sole Proprietor	Yes	Yes	1099-NEC/1099-K
Movers	Corporation	Yes	No	1099-K
Legal Services	Corporation	Yes	Yes	1099-K
CPA	S. Corporation	Yes	Yes	1099-K
Computer Repair	LLC	Yes	Yes	1099-NEC/1099-K
Parking lot	LLP	Yes	No	1099-K

*LLP's and Corporations usually don't not get 1099's, but if they used a 3rd party processor they could get a 1099-K. If you are a lawyer and received payment for legal services you will get a 1099-NEC. When you get your 1099's compare the amounts and client name to be sure. Some 1099-Ks will be lumped together i.e. all PayPal transactions etc.

Be careful when you are a contractor that receives a 1099-K. You don't want to get a 1099-K from the 3rd party and a 1099-NEC from the business owner. It should be one 1099 or the other.

Quiz: What do you know about 1099s?

1. Jeri is a makeup and hair stylist. She doesn't have a shop and hustles ads on social media and Craigslist. She has eight clients that paid $28,022 with Paypal. Which 1099 will she get?

1099-MISC ___
1099-K ___
1099-NEC ___
None ___

2. Ron is a web designer. He has a home office and has two clients who paid $9,050 with Venmo. Which 1099 will he get?

1099-MISC ___
1099-K ___
1099-NEC ___
None ___

3. Jake is an eBay seller and he works from home. He earned $21,050 selling on eBay only. Which 1099 will he get?

1099-MISC ___
1099-K ___
1099-NEC ___
None ___

4. Ashley is a sole proprietor and received 68,000 through Zelle for business transactions. Will she get a 1099?

NO ___
YES ___

5. Bob and Joe have a partnership. They don't like paying fees for so they only accept checks. Which type of 1099s are they likely to receive from?

1099-MISC ___
1099-K ___
1099-NEC ___
None ___

6. Tim is a driver for Uber. He earned $13,615 in 2021. Which 1099 will he get?

1099-MISC ___
1099-K ___
1099-NEC ___
None ___

7. Rick is a driver for Lyft. He earned $12,461 in 2021. Which 1099 will he get?

1099-MISC ___
1099-K ___
1099-NEC ___
None ___

8. James and Elva have a food truck and only take cash and 50% Square. What 1099 will they receive?

1099-MISC ___
1099-K ___
1099-NEC ___
None ___

9. Janise is a bookkeeper and earned $54,563.15 in 2021. She uses Paypal for payments. What 1099 will she get?

1099-MISC ___
1099-K ___
1099-NEC ___
None ___

10. Terry is a sole proprietor of a cleaning company. She earned $42,062 in 2021. She has one client who pays by check. What 1099 will she get?

1099-MISC ___
1099-K ___
1099-NEC ___
None ___

11. Bobbi is an Los Angeles Etsy seller. She earned $12,461 in 2021. What 1099 will she get?

1099-MISC___
1099-K ___
1099-NEC ___

12. Josie is an AirBnB host. She received 27,038 dollars. Which 1099 will she get?

1099-MISC ___
1099-K ___
1099-NEC ___
None ___

13. Sam tells Julie her work days and time. He tells her exactly what her job entails and how to do it. Is Julie an employee or self-employed?

Self-employed ___
Employee ___
Neither ___
Both ___

14. Robert is a gets a payroll check every two weeks. Is Robert an employee self-employed?

Self-employed ___
Employee ___
Neither ___
Both ___

15. Lee moves furniture and gets paid cash after every gig. Is Lee an employee or self-employed?

Self-employed ___
Employee ___
Neither ___
Both ___

 CONTINUED ON NEXT PAGE

Quiz continued

16. Louis can repair anything and has an ad on Craigslist for his services. Is Louis an employee or self-employed?

Self-employed ___
Employee ___
Neither ___
Both ___

17. Fran is an awesome baker and sells cakes and pies to friends. Is she an employee or self-employed?

Self-employed ___
Employee ___
Neither ___
Both ___

18. Michelle clocks in every morning at 8am and takes lunch at noon. Is Michelle an employee or self-employed?

Self-employed ___
Employee ___
Neither ___
Both ___

19. Mario is a tattoo artist and people flock to him. Is Mario an employee or self-employed?

Self-employed ___
Employee ___

Neither ___
Both ___

20. Angel is an receptionist paid. She works forty hours per week and takes a vacation. Is Angel an employee or self-employed?

Self-employed ___
Employee ___
Neither ___
Both ___

21. Jalen has three gigs and gets paid cash. Does Jalen still have to report his gig money to the IRS?

Yes ___
No ___

22. Bob gets cash for moping floors on the weekends. Does Bob have to report the money he received to the IRS?

Yes ___
No ___

23. Rick begs for money and gets over $50 per day. Does Rick have to report the cash he receives to the IRS?

Yes ___
No ___

Quiz Answers

1. 1099-K
2. 1099-K
3. 1099-K
4. No - Zelle does not give 1099-Ks
5. 1099-NEC
6. 1099-K
7. 1099-K
8. 1099-K
9. 1099-K
10. 1099-NEC
11. 1099-K
12. 1099-K
13. Employee
14. Employee
15. Self-employed
16. Self-employed
17. Self-employed
18. Employee
19. Self-employed
20. Employee
21. Yes
22. Yes
23. Yes

Continued from page 20

Frequently Asked

Q. Do I have to report 1099-K income?
Yes because if you got the form then the IRS know about you.

Q. I sold some stuff on eBay and Esty. Will I get a 1099?
You will receive a 1099-K form from eBay, and Etsy if you had sales over $600.

Q. 1099-MISC vs. Form 1099-K: What's the Difference?
The 1099-MISC reports income from checks and cash received. The 1099-K form reports bank card income from all your customers and clients.

Q. What if I lose my 1099?
Call the company and ask for a replacement.

Q. What if I ignore my 1099s I received?
The IRS will send you a estimated bill.

Form W-9
Rev. October 2018
Department of the Treasury
Internal Revenue Service

Request for Taxpayer
Identification Number and Certification

▶ Go to www.irs.gov/FormW9 for instructions and the latest information.

Give Form to the requester. Do not send to the IRS.

1 Name (as shown on your income tax return). Name is required on this line; do not leave this line blank.

MAX EXAMPLE

2 Business name/disregarded entity name, if different from above

3 Check appropriate box for federal tax classification of the person whose name is entered on line 1. Check only **one** of the following seven boxes.

- ☑ Individual/sole proprietor or single-member LLC
- ☐ C Corporation
- ☐ S Corporation
- ☐ Partnership
- ☐ Trust/estate

☐ Limited liability company. Enter the tax classification (C=C corporation, S=S corporation, P=Partnership) ▶ _____

Note: Check the appropriate box in the line above for the tax classification of the single-member owner. Do not check LLC if the LLC is classified as a single-member LLC that is disregarded from the owner unless the owner of the LLC is another LLC that is **not** disregarded from the owner for U.S. federal tax purposes. Otherwise, a single-member LLC that is disregarded from the owner should check the appropriate box for the tax classification of its owner.

☐ Other (see instructions) ▶

4 Exemptions (codes apply only to certain entities, not individuals; see instructions on page 3):

Exempt payee code (if any) _____

Exemption from FATCA reporting code (if any) _____

(Applies to accounts maintained outside the U.S.)

5 Address (number, street, and apt. or suite no.) See instructions.

705 SOMERS AVE

6 City, state, and ZIP code

LOS ANGELES, CA 90012

Requester's name and address (optional)

7 List account number(s) here (optional)

Part I — Taxpayer Identification Number (TIN)

Enter your TIN in the appropriate box. The TIN provided must match the name given on line 1 to avoid backup withholding. For individuals, this is generally your social security number (SSN). However, for a resident alien, sole proprietor, or disregarded entity, see the instructions for Part I, later. For other entities, it is your employer identification number (EIN). If you do not have a number, see How to get a TIN, later.

Note: If the account is in more than one name, see the instructions for line 1. Also see What Name and Number To Give the Requester for guidelines on whose number to enter.

Social security number: 5 4 6 – 2 1 – 1 5 2 3

or

Employer identification number:

Part II — Certification

Under penalties of perjury, I certify that:

1. The number shown on this form is my correct taxpayer identification number (or I am waiting for a number to be issued to me); and
2. I am not subject to backup withholding because: (a) I am exempt from backup withholding, or (b) I have not been notified by the Internal Revenue Service (IRS) that I am subject to backup withholding as a result of a failure to report all interest or dividends, or (c) the IRS has notified me that I am no longer subject to backup withholding; and
3. I am a U.S. citizen or other U.S. person (defined below); and
4. The FATCA code(s) entered on this form (if any) indicating that I am exempt from FATCA reporting is correct.

Certification instructions. You must cross out item 2 above if you have been notified by the IRS that you are currently subject to backup withholding because you have failed to report all interest and dividends on your tax return. For real estate transactions, item 2 does not apply. For mortgage interest paid, acquisition or abandonment of secured property, cancellation of debt, contributions to an individual retirement arrangement (IRA), and generally, payments other than interest and dividends, you are not required to sign the certification, but you must provide your correct TIN. See the instructions for Part II, later.

Sign Here
Signature of U.S. person ▶ **MAX EXAMPLE**
Date ▶ **3/12/2023**

Download form www.irs.gov/pub/irs-pdf/fw9.pdf

For each client you work with, you will need to complete a W-9 form. The completed form will be kept on file by your client and will not be sent to the IRS. If you have a business name and EIN, be sure to provide that information on the form. It is important to select the appropriate entity type, such as "sole proprietor," as this information will be used to generate your 1099-NEC and 1099-MISC forms. In addition, third-party companies may also require you to fill out a W-9 form.

"Form 1099-K: The 3rd party keeps a copy, you get a copy and the IRS gets a copy"

☐ CORRECTED (if checked)

FILER'S name, street address, city or town, state or province, country, ZIP or foreign postal code, and telephone no.	FILER'S TIN	OMB No. 1545-2205	
INTERNET SALES, INC. 1223 TARGET STREEET, SUITE 432 LOS ANGELES, CA 90605	45-25472215	Form **1099-K**	**Payment Card and Third Party Network Transactions**
	PAYEE'S TIN ***-**-1523	(Rev. January 2022)	
	1a Gross amount of payment card/third party network transactions $ 16,845.22	For calendar year 20 22	
	1b Card Not Present transactions $ 16,845.22	2 Merchant category code 1255	**Copy B**
Check to indicate if FILER is a (an): ☐ Payment settlement entity (PSE) ✔ Electronic Payment Facilitator (EPF)/Other third party ☐	Check to indicate transactions reported are: ☐ Payment card ✔ Third party network	**For Payee**
		3 Number of payment transactions 424	4 Federal income tax withheld $	This is important tax information and is being furnished to the IRS. If you are required to file a return, a negligence penalty or other sanction may be imposed on you if taxable income results from this transaction and the IRS determines that it has not been reported.
PAYEE'S name MAX EXAMPLE	5a January $ 1,300.25	5b February $ 1,554.14	
	5c March $ 1,046.05	5d April $ 1,745.22	
Street address (including apt. no.) 705 SOMERS AVE	5e May $ 1,562.25	5f June $ 1,183.16	
	5g July $ 1,665.23	5h August $ 1,702.31	
City or town, state or province, country, and ZIP or foreign postal code LOS ANGELES, CA 90012	5i September $ 1,098.22	5j October $ 1,672.15	
PSE'S name and telephone number MERCHANT SERVICES, INC (888) 261-1722	5k November $ 1,088.25	5l December $ 1,227.99	
Account number (see instructions) ACCT#225-5557	6 State - - - - - - - - -	7 State identification no. - - - - - - - - -	8 State income tax withheld $ $

Form **1099-K** (Rev. 1-2022) Keep for your records) www.irs.gov/Form1099K Department of the Treasury - Internal Revenue Service

www.irs.gov/pub/irs-pdf/f1099k.pdf

The purpose of the IRS Form 1099-K is to report payment card and third-party network transactions to the Internal Revenue Service (IRS) and to taxpayers. This form reports the total amount of payment card transactions, such as credit and debit card transactions, processed by a third-party payment settlement organization on behalf of a business and starting in 2024 it will apply to individuals as well.

It is used by the IRS to monitor compliance with tax laws and to ensure that business owners and individuals are reporting all of their taxable income.

Form 1099-NEC: The Business Owner keeps a copy, you get a copy and the IRS gets a copy

☐ CORRECTED (if checked)

PAYER'S name, street address, city or town, state or province, country, ZIP or foreign postal code, and telephone no.		OMB No. 1545-0116	
JOE SIMS WORK SHOES		Form **1099-NEC**	**Nonemployee Compensation**
2211 ROCKWELL AVE		(Rev. January 2022)	
LOS ANGELES, CA 90042		For calendar year 20 **22**	

PAYER'S TIN	RECIPIENT'S TIN	1 Nonemployee compensation	Copy B
35-12447113	***-**-1523	$ 2,400	**For Recipient**
RECIPIENT'S name		2 Payer made direct sales totaling $5,000 or more of consumer products to recipient for resale ☐	This is important tax information and is being furnished to the IRS. If you are required to file a return, a negligence penalty or other sanction may be imposed on you if this income is taxable and the IRS determines that it has not been reported.
MAX EXAMPLE		3	
Street address (including apt. no.)			
705 SOMERS AVE		4 Federal income tax withheld	
City or town, state or province, country, and ZIP or foreign postal code		$	
LOS ANGELES, CA 90012		5 State tax withheld	6 State/Payer's state no.	7 State income
Account number (see instructions)		$		$
		$		$

Form **1099-NEC** (Rev. 1-2022)　　keep for your records)　　www.irs.gov/Form1099NEC　　Department of the Treasury - Internal Revenue Service

www.irs.gov/pub/irs-pdf/f1099nec.pdf

The 1099-NEC is a simple form and most people who get paid by check, wire, or direct deposit from a business will most likely get this form. Remember you get a copy, the business keeps a copy and a copy goes to the IRS.

The 1099-NEC form from the business owner tells the IRS you got paid! If after reading this guide, and the business owner does not have you fill out a W-9 you might not get a 1099-NEC.

It's your responsibility to give the business owner a W-9 and 1099-NEC if you earned more than $600.

This is just in case the IRS needs proof of your income. You don't want the IRS snooping around your bank account!

Form 1099-MISC: The Business Owner keeps a copy, you get a copy and the IRS gets a copy

PAYER'S name, street address, city or town, state or province, country, ZIP or foreign postal code, and telephone no.		1 Rents $	OMB No. 1545-0115 Form **1099-MISC** (Rev. January 2022) For calendar year 20 __22__	**Miscellaneous Information**
LIVE ENTERTAINMENT, INC 2881 BURBANK BLVD BURBANK, CA 91505		2 Royalties $		
		3 Other income $ 2,350	4 Federal income tax withheld $	**Copy B** For Recipient
PAYER'S TIN 64 85881124	RECIPIENT'S TIN ···1523	5 Fishing boat proceeds $	6 Medical and health care payments $	
RECIPIENT'S name MAX EXAMPLE		7 Payer made direct sales totaling $5,000 or more of consumer products to recipient for resale ☐	8 Substitute payments in lieu of dividends or interest $	This is important tax information and is being furnished to the IRS. If you are required to file a return, a negligence penalty or other sanction may be imposed on you if this income is taxable and the IRS determines that it has not been reported.
Street address (including apt. no.) 705 SOMERS AVE		9 Crop insurance proceeds $	10 Gross proceeds paid to an attorney $	
City or town, state or province, country, and ZIP or foreign postal code LOS ANGELES, CA 90012		11 Fish purchased for resale $	12 Section 409A deferrals $	
	13 FATCA filing requirement ☐	14 Excess golden parachute payments $	15 Nonqualified deferred compensation $	
Account number (see instructions)		16 State tax withheld $ $	17 State/Payer's state no.	18 State income $ $

Form **1099-MISC** (Rev. 1-2022)   (keep for your records)   www.irs.gov/Form1099MISC   Department of the Treasury - Internal Revenue Service

www.irs.gov/pub/irs-pdf/f1099msc.pdf

The IRS Form 1099-MISC is used to report miscellaneous income to the Internal Revenue Service (IRS) and to taxpayers. This form is used to report income received by a person for work performed as an independent contractor, rent, prizes, and awards, among other types of miscellaneous income.

Businesses and organizations are required to file a 1099-MISC for each person to whom they have paid at least $600 in a tax year for services rendered or for rent and payment is usually paid by check. The form is used by the IRS to verify that taxpayers are reporting all of their taxable income and to ensure compliance with tax laws.

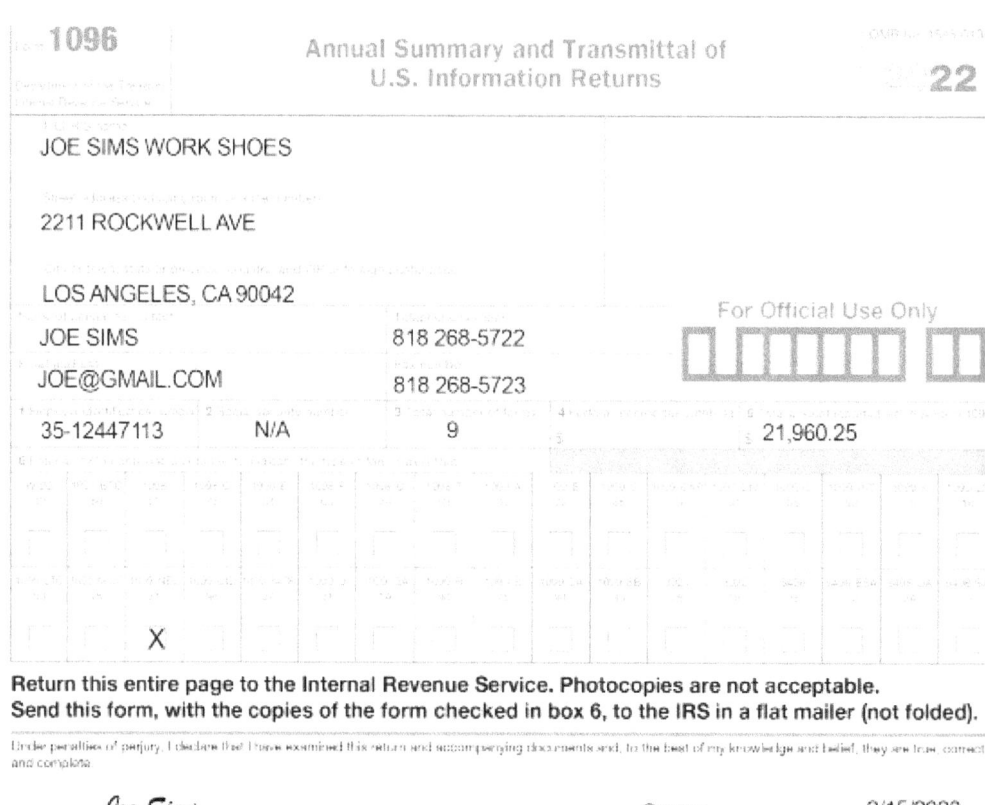

1096

Annual Summary and Transmittal of U.S. Information Returns

22

JOE SIMS WORK SHOES

2211 ROCKWELL AVE

LOS ANGELES, CA 90042

JOE SIMS   818 268-5722

JOE@GMAIL.COM   818 268-5723

For Official Use Only

| 35-12447113 | N/A | 9 | | 21,960.25 |

X

**Return this entire page to the Internal Revenue Service. Photocopies are not acceptable.
Send this form, with the copies of the form checked in box 6, to the IRS in a flat mailer (not folded).**

Under penalties of perjury, I declare that I have examined this return and accompanying documents and, to the best of my knowledge and belief, they are true, correct and complete.

Signature ► *Joe Sims*   Title ► Owner   Date ► 2/15/2023

www.irs.gov/pub/irs-pdf/f1096.pdf

The purpose of the 1096 Form is to reconcile 1099-MISC or 1099-NEC forms. In Joe's case, he distributed nine 1099-NEC forms, and if he had any 1099-MISC forms, he would report them separately on a distinct 1096 Form. To simplify the process, contractors only need to complete the W-9 form, while business owners are responsible for filing the 1099 forms. The total number of 1099 forms must match the total reported on the 1096 Form.

It is important to note that the form available on the IRS website can not be used. Instead, one must purchase the required forms or use a service provider such as www.greatland.com to file each form for $5 which can save time.

About the Author
Steph Wynne

THANK YOU FOR READING!

I love to read and write!

It hasn't always been that way. As I got older I
realized that I was a "learner."
With learning came reading and writing!

Now I can't stop!

Steph wants her words to be read 100 years from
now and resides in Los Angeles, California.

You can find Steph's books on Amazon or